BASIC / NOT BORING MATH SKILLS

DECIMALS

Grades 6–8[+]

Inventive Exercises to Sharpen Skills and Raise Achievement

Series Concept & Development
by Imogene Forte & Marjorie Frank
Exercises by Marjorie Frank

Incentive Publications, Inc.
Nashville, Tennessee

About the cover:
Bound resist, or tie dye, is the most ancient known method of fabric surface design. The brilliance of the basic tie dye design on this cover reflects the possibilities that emerge from the mastery of basic skills.

Illustrated by Kathleen Bullock
Cover art by Mary Patricia Deprez, dba Tye Dye Mary®
Cover design by Marta Drayton, Joe Shibley, and W. Paul Nance
Edited by Jennifer J. Streams

ISBN 0-86530-503-X

1   2   3   4   5   6   7   8   9   10   08   07   06   05

PRINTED IN THE UNITED STATES OF AMERICA
www.incentivepublications.com

TABLE OF CONTENTS

CELEBRATE BASIC MATH SKILLS

Basic does not mean boring! There certainly is nothing dull about using decimals to . . .

> . . . solve tricky problems about the ancient and modern Olympic games
>
> . . . compare the speed of the fastest man to the fastest avalanche
>
> . . . find out about record basketball dribbles, steals, blocks, and points
>
> . . . discover who can jump farther—a frog, flea, or Olympic athlete
>
> . . . divide decimals as a karate expert divides blocks of wood with bare hands
>
> . . . get to know the salaries of the world's top-earning athletes
>
> . . . follow Olympic kayakers through wild rapids to calculate their speeds

The idea of celebrating the basics is just what it sounds like—enjoying and improving the basic skills of solving math problems. The pages that follow are full of exercises that will help students to review and strengthen specific, basic skills in the content area of math. This is not just another "fill-in-the-blanks" way to learn. The high-interest exercises will put students to work applying a rich variety of the most important math skills while enjoying fun and challenging adventures with numbers, ideas, amazing feats, and world sports records.

The pages in this book can be used in many ways:

- for individual students to review or practice a particular skill
- with a small group needing to relearn or strengthen a skill
- as an instructional tool for teaching a skill to any size group
- by students working on their own
- by students working under the direction of an adult

Each page may be used to introduce a new skill, reinforce a skill, or assess a student's ability to perform a skill. And, there's more to the book than just the great student activities! You'll also find a hearty appendix of resources helpful for students and teachers—including a ready-to-use test for assessing these problem solving skills.

As students take on the challenges of these word adventures, they will grow in their mastery of basic skills and will enjoy themselves while they learn. And as you watch them check off the basic skills they've strengthened, you can celebrate with them!

The Skills Test (pages 56–59)
Use the skills test as a pretest and/or post-test. This will help you check the students' mastery of basic language arts skills, and prepare them for success on tests of standards, instructional goals, or other individual achievement.

SKILLS CHECKLIST FOR DECIMALS

✔	SKILL	PAGE(S)
	Read decimal numerals	10, 11
	Write decimals with words	10, 11, 13
	Write decimal numerals	12, 13
	Read and write mixed decimal numerals	14, 15
	Compare decimals	16, 17
	Order decimals	17
	Identify place value in decimals	18–21
	Round decimals	20, 21
	Add or subtract decimals	22, 23
	Multiply decimals	24, 25, 28
	Divide decimals	26, 27, 29
	Multiply and divide decimals by multiples of ten	28, 29
	Solve problems with decimals	30, 31
	Operations with decimal integers	32
	Solve problems with decimal integers	32, 33
	Scientific notation	34, 35
	Change fractions to decimals; change decimals to fractions	36, 37
	Write decimals as percent and percent as decimals	38, 39
	Find what percent a number is of another number; find base numbers	40, 41
	Find percent of a number	40–45
	Solve problems with percent	40–45
	Solve consumer problems involving interest, tax, and discounts	44, 45, 47
	Complete operations with money	46, 47
	Solve problems with money	47
	Identify repeating and terminating decimals	48

Decimals

Skills Exercises

BACK TO ATHENS

Athens, the capital of Greece, hosted the first modern Olympic games in 1896. The games returned to Athens 108 years later, in 2004. Over 10,500 athletes represented about 200 nations.

Read some decimals connected to the events at the Athens games.

Circle the correct answer.

1. The estimated cost of the Athens games was one and five tenths billion dollars. This decimal numeral is:

   a. $ 15.0 billion   b. $1.510 billion   c. $1.5 billion   d. $1.05 billion   e. $1.005 billion

2. 790 medals were given at the games. The U.S. won 103 medals. This was thirteen and three hundred eighty ten-thousandths percent of the total. This decimal numeral is:

   a. 13.0380%   b. 13.380%   c. 13.30080%   d. 13.038%

3. Seven and seventy-seven hundredths percent of the U.S. medals were won by swimmer Michael Phelps. His 8 medals tied a record for the most medals won in a single Olympics. This decimal numeral is:

   a. 7.77%   b. 7.077%   c. 7.777%   d. 7.707%

4. 10,500 athletes participated in the Athens games. 24 were expelled for drug use. This was two hundred twenty-nine thousandths percent of the total athletes. This decimal numeral is:

   a. 2.229%   b. 0.0229%   c. 0.229%   d. 0.00229%

5. Yuliya Nesterenko of Belarus won the 100-meter women's run in ten and ninety-three hundredths seconds. This decimal numeral is:

   a. 10.93   b. 10.093   c. 1.093   d. 1.903

6. Justin Gatlin, U.S., won the 100-meter men's run in nine and eighty-five hundredths seconds. This decimal numeral is:

   a. 9.805   b. 9.85   c. 9.085   d. 9.0085

Use with page 11.

Name

A U.S. team won the men's 1600-meter relay in 19.01 seconds.
Written in words, this decimal number reads:

nineteen and one hundredth seconds

Match the numerals to the correct words.

____ 1. 0.0035 a. thirty-two hundredths

____ 2. 0.235 b. thirty-two hundred-thousandths

____ 3. 0.007 c. seven thousandths

____ 4. 0.07 d. three hundred fifty-five thousandths

____ 5. 0.707 e. thirty-five ten-thousandths

____ 6. 0.32 f. seven hundredths

____ 7. 0.00032 g. two hundred thirty-five thousandths

____ 8. 0.355 h. seven hundred seven thousandths

Camelia Potec of Romania won the women's 200-meter freestyle swimming competition
in 1:58.03. Written in words, this number reads:

one minute, fifty-eight and three hundredths seconds

Match the words to the correct numeral.

____ 9. six hundred-thousandths

____ 10. four hundred four thousandths

____ 11. eighty-eight thousandths

____ 12. six thousandths

____ 13. eighty-eight hundredths

____ 14. four hundred four ten-thousandths

____ 15. seven hundredths

i. 0.0404
j. 0.088
k. 0.0088
l. 0.7
m. 0.00006
n. 0.07
o. 700
p. 0.404
q. 0.88
r. 0.0006
s. 0.006

Use with page 10.

Name

SEVEN GREAT FEATS

The heptathlon is an athletic event that actually includes seven separate track and field events. Jacqueline Joyner-Kersee (USA) set a world record in 1988 by scoring a total of 7,291 points.

Write the correct decimal numeral to match the words.

_____ 1. Jackie Joyner-Kersee threw the javelin **forty-five and sixty-six hundredths** meters.

_____ 2. The high jump distance for Jackie was **seventy-three and twenty-five hundredths** inches.

_____ 3. The rate of Jackie's 800-meter run was just under **six and two thousand sixteen ten-thousandths** meters per second.

_____ 4. Jackie ran the 200-meter in 22.56 seconds. This means her rate was about **eight and eight hundred sixty-five thousandths** meters per second.

_____ 5. Her time in the 100-meter hurdles was **twelve and sixty-nine hundredths** seconds.

_____ 6. Her distance for the shot put event was **fifteen and eight tenths** meters.

_____ 7. In the long jump event, Jackie jumped **seven and twenty-seven hundredths** meters.

Write the correct decimal numeral to match the words.

_____ 8. five hundred sixteen thousandths

_____ 9. three thousandths

_____ 10. five ten thousandths

_____ 11. sixty-two thousandths

_____ 12. eleven hundred-thousandths

_____ 13. nine hundred thirty-four thousandths

_____ 14. eighty-nine hundredths

_____ 15. eight hundredths

_____ 16. nine hundred-thousandths

_____ 17. two hundred nine ten-thousandths

_____ 18. six thousand two ten-thousandths

I'll perform the feat with my fleeting feet!

Name _____

AMAZING FOOTWORK

There are all kinds of races that get athletes moving on their feet. Some involve running. Some involve walking. Some of the races are rather unusual.

Write the decimal number in words.

1. Ashrita Furman of the U.S.A holds the record for the fastest skipping marathon. His rate was about **4.3333** miles per hour.

   _____

   _____

2. The record for the fastest 100-meter backwards walk is held by Ferdie Adoboe of Ghana. The rate of his walk was **0.136** meters per second.

   _____

3. The fastest finish in a 3-legged marathon is credited to a set of twins. Nick and Alastair Benbow (UK) won the race with a time of **3.67** hours.

   _____

4. Han Frenken (Netherlands) holds the record for the fastest baby-carriage pushing marathon. He finished the race in about **3.9** hours.

   _____

Write the words to match each decimal.

5. 0.91 _____

6. 0.7 _____

7. 0.436 _____

8. 0. 00002 _____

9. 0.0101 _____

10. 0.2022 _____

11. 0.66 _____

12. 0.008 _____

Name _____

DECIMALS ON THE COURT

Basketball records are the topic here. Practice your skills at reading mixed decimal numbers while you find out about some skilled accomplishments on the courts.

Are the words correct? Write **yes** or **no**.

_____ 1. In the 1961–1962 NBA season, player Wilt Chamberlain set a record for the highest average of points scored per game. That average was **50.4** points per game. Is this mixed decimal number: **fifty and four hundredths**?

_____ 2. The greatest number of blocks in an NBA career is 3,830 in 1,238 games. The player who set this record is Hakeem Olajuwon. This averages out to **3.09** blocks per game. Is this mixed decimal number: **three and nine thousandths**?

_____ 3. Australian player Suresh Joachim dribbled a basketball **156.71** kilometers in 24 hours. This is the greatest distance a basketball has been dribbled in a 24-hour period. Is this mixed decimal number: **one hundred fifty-six and seventy-one hundredths**?

_____ 4. John Stockton holds the record for the most steals in an NBA career. The average was **2.1709** per game. Is this mixed decimal number: **two and one hundred seventy-nine thousandths**?

_____ 5. The most fouls made in an NBA career totaled 4,657. Kareem Abdul-Jabbar holds this record. He averaged **2.983** fouls per game in his 1,560-game career. Is this mixed decimal numeral: **two and nine hundred eighty-three ten-thousandths**?

Which one?

Circle the letter of the correct words to match the numeral.

6. Average game time in a 27-game marathon: **0.985** hours
   a. nine hundred eighty-five ten thousandths
   b. nine hundred eighty-five thousandths
   c. nine and eighty-five hundredths

7. Most rebounds in NBA career: average **22.8937** per game
   a. twenty-two and eight thousand nine hundred thirty-seven hundred-thousandths
   b. twenty-two and eight thousand nine hundred thirty-seven thousandths
   c. twenty-two and eight thousand nine hundred thirty-seven ten thousandths

Name

DECIMALS OFF THE COURT

Decimals play a part in the lives of players off the basketball court, too. Circle the right decimal numerals to match the word version of each number.

1. Naomi snacks on an energy bar that weighs five and twelve hundredths ounces. This is:
   a. 5.012
   b. 0.512
   c. 5.12

2. After every practice, she drinks two and seven hundredths liters of water. This is:
   a. 2.70
   b. 20.7
   c. 2.07

3. When she launders her uniform, it takes twenty-three and seven hundredths minutes for the shorts to dry. This is:
   a. 23.70
   b. 23.07
   c. 23.7

4. Naomi weighs one hundred twenty-two and eight tenths pounds. This is:
   a. 122.8
   b. 122.08
   c. 122.008

5. The exact mileage to the gym from Naomi's home is four and fifty-five thousandths miles. This is:
   a. 4.0055
   b. 4.0505
   c. 4.055

6. Naomi eats a scrambled egg every morning. It takes the egg two and seven hundredths minutes to cook. This is:
   a. 20.7
   b. 2.007
   c. 2.07

7. When she goes out for a walk, her stride is two and sixty-six thousandths feet. This is:
   a. 2.066
   b. 0.266
   c. 2.66

8. Her pet dachshund is exactly fourteen and fourteen ten-thousandths inches long. This is:
   a. 14.14
   b. 14.014
   c. 14.0014

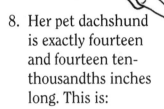

9. She is the taller than any other member of her basketball team by three and ninety-two thousandths inches. This is:
   a. 3.92
   b. 3.092
   c. 3.0092

10. Naomi can eat a small pizza in six and one hundred four ten-thousandths minutes. This is:
    a. 6.0104
    b. 6.104
    c. 6.14

Name

JUMPING HIGH

The world high jump record for men is 2.45 meters. The women's record is 2.09 meters. Compare these athletes' jumps registered in a day-long practice session.

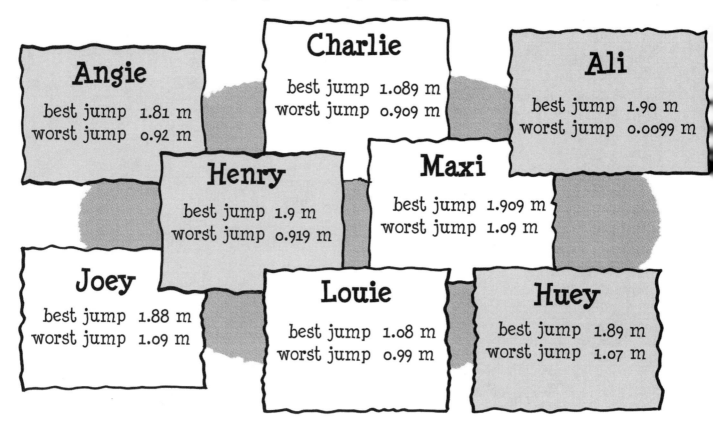

Angie
best jump   1.81 m
worst jump   0.92 m

Charlie
best jump   1.089 m
worst jump   0.909 m

Ali
best jump   1.90 m
worst jump   0.0099 m

Henry
best jump   1.9 m
worst jump   0.919 m

Maxi
best jump   1.909 m
worst jump   1.09 m

Joey
best jump   1.88 m
worst jump   1.09 m

Louie
best jump   1.08 m
worst jump   0.99 m

Huey
best jump   1.89 m
worst jump   1.07 m

Write an expression that describes each comparison. Use the symbols <, >, or =. For example: write 1.029 > 1.009.

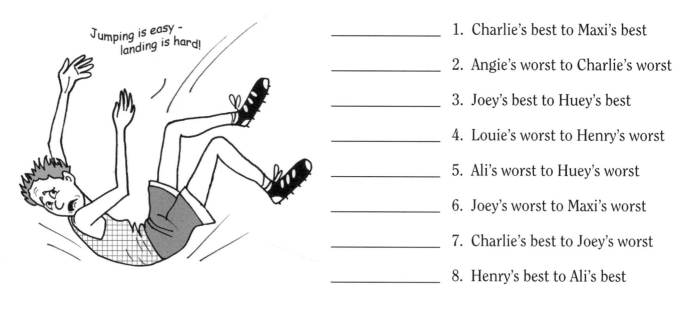

Jumping is easy – landing is hard!

_____ 1. Charlie's best to Maxi's best

_____ 2. Angie's worst to Charlie's worst

_____ 3. Joey's best to Huey's best

_____ 4. Louie's worst to Henry's worst

_____ 5. Ali's worst to Huey's worst

_____ 6. Joey's worst to Maxi's worst

_____ 7. Charlie's best to Joey's worst

_____ 8. Henry's best to Ali's best

Name _____

JUMPING LONG

Mike Powell (USA) holds the world record for the men's long jump (8.95 m).
The women's record is held by Galena Christyakova of the former USSR (7.52 m).

Use the table to compare the jumps and other statistics of these athletes.

Athlete	Best Jump meters	Time from Home to the Track minutes	Weights pounds	Height inches	Time to Get Up from the Last Jump minutes
J. Lane	8.37	4.09	105.07	65.3	0.212
T. McCall	8.702	16.32	109.9	66.009	0.202
V. Annan	8.07	16.091	109.09	65.003	0.1902
C. Tooey	8.655	4.019	105.707	64.107	0.109
R. Ruiz	8.669	4.1	105.097	66.091	0.602

Write the order from the least to the greatest distance, weight, length, or time.
Give the answer by writing the initials of the athletes.

1. Order according to best jump.   ____, ____, ____, ____, ____

2. Order according to weights.   ____, ____, ____, ____, ____

3. Order according to time from home to track.   ____, ____, ____, ____, ____

4. Order according to time to get up from last jump. ____, ____, ____, ____, ____

5. Order according to heights.   ____, ____, ____, ____, ____

Jumps
Athlete:

A 7.07 m   **F** 7.071 m

B 7.707 m   **G** 7.777 m

C 7.717 m   **H** 7.107 m

D 7.0777 m   **I** 7.0707 m

E 7.007 m

6. Which had the jump in the middle (median)? ____

7. Which athlete jumped farthest? ____

8. Which had the shortest jump? ____

Geronimo!

Name _____

     17

BY LEAPS AND BOUNDS

Sharpen your skills at identifying place value with these facts about some amazing jumpers.
Tell the place value of the bold digit in each measurement.

1. In 1987, Stefka Kostadinova set the world high jump record for women with a 2.0**9** m jump.

   Place value of 9: _____

2. A 10 cm long desert rat can jump 46 times its body length—a distance of 4.572 m.

   Place value of 2: _____

3. An Asian grasshopper can jump 18 times its body length—a distance of 4.5**7**2 m.

   Place value of 5:

   _____

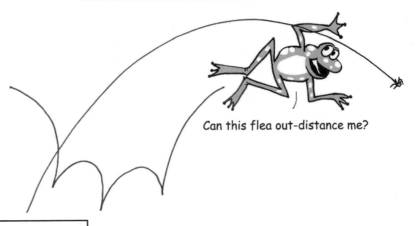

Can this flea out-distance me?

4. The common flea can jump 220 times its body size—a distance of 33.0**2** cm.

   Place value of 0: _____

5. A goliath frog can jump 10 times its body length—a distance of 3.04**8** m.

   Place value of 8: _____

6. **0.000385**   What is the place value of the 8? _____

7. **79.703**   What is the place value of the 0? _____

8. **500.7193**   What is the place value of the 9? _____

9. **1996.05**   What is the place value of the 1? _____

10. **300.902**   What is the place value of the 9? _____

11. **4.00035**   What is the place value of the 4? _____

12. **82,704.6**   What is the place value of the 6? _____

13. **0.03728**   What is the place value of the 2? _____

14. **1922.7**   What is the place value of the 9? _____

Name _____

EVENTS OF SPEED

Enjoy reading these fascinating speed facts.

Then complete the table by writing (in words) the value of the place of the identified digit.

I'm not sure that this will be a fair race. What do you think?

It sure looks fishy to me.

Event	Speed	Digit	Value of the Place
1. Fastest cycling in snow	212.139 k/h	9	
2. Fastest yacht speed	53.56 mi/h	6	
3. Fastest air speed	2193.17 mi/h	9	
4. Fastest land speed	763.035 mi/h	5	
5. Fastest skydiving speed	325.67 mi/h	6	
6. Fastest un-paced 1-km cycling	58.875 k/sec	7	
7. Fastest 100 meters on a unicycle	29.72 k/h	9	
8. Fastest avalanche speed	402.3 k/h	4	
9. Fastest passenger elevator	22.72 mi/h	7	
10. Caterpillar speed	38.1 cm/sec	3	
11. Fastest fish (sailfish)	1.1444 mi/min	4 (last)	
12. Fastest man (Tim Montgomery)	10.22494 m/sec	9	
13. Fastest worm-eating	3.1333 worms/sec	1	
14. Fastest sheep-shearing	58.25 sheep/h	8	
15. Snail speed	0.05 k/h	0	

Name

ALL-AROUND ROUNDING

The most important event in gymnastics is the all-around, where an individual's scores on each apparatus (plus their floor exercise score) are added together to find the best complete gymnast.

Use these gymnastic scores in the all-around and other events to practice rounding decimals.

1.
2004 Olympic champion gymnast Paul Hamm received a score of **57.823** points. Round this to the nearest hundredth.

_____

2.
The silver medalist in 2004 was South Korean Kim Dae Eun. His score was **57.811**. Round this to the nearest tenth.

_____

3.
The bronze medal was won by Korean Yang Tae Young. His score was **57.774**. Round this to the nearest ten.

_____

4.
American Brett McClure scored **9.162** on the still rings in the 2004 Olympics. Round this to the nearest tenth.

_____

5.
The U.S. Men's Gymnastic Team won a silver medal in team competition. Their score was **172.933**. Round this to the nearest ten.

_____

6.
The final score for the German team at the 2004 Olympics was **167.372**. Round this to the nearest hundredth.

_____

7.
Pasakevi Voula Kouna, of Greece, is the youngest gymnast to compete internationally. She was **9.81917** years old. Round this to the nearest ten-thousandth.

_____

8.
Of the top 11 male all-time medal winners in Summer Olympics, **54.545454%** are gymnasts. Round this decimal to the nearest hundredth.

_____

Name

MORNING ROUND UP

Each morning, gymnast Anna blends up a special, nutritious drink that's full of decimals.
Use her recipe for practicing your rounding skills.

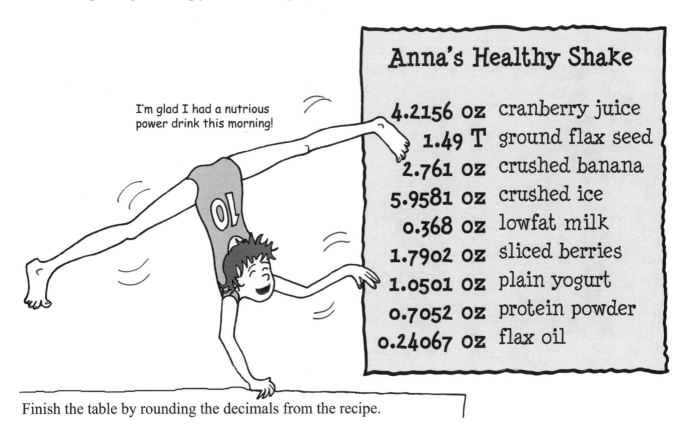

I'm glad I had a nutrious power drink this morning!

Anna's Healthy Shake

4.2156 oz cranberry juice
1.49 T ground flax seed
2.761 oz crushed banana
5.9581 oz crushed ice
0.368 oz lowfat milk
1.7902 oz sliced berries
1.0501 oz plain yogurt
0.7052 oz protein powder
0.24067 oz flax oil

Finish the table by rounding the decimals from the recipe.

	rounded to	answer	rounded to	answer
1. juice	nearest hundredth		nearest thousandth	
2. flax seed	nearest ones		nearest tenth	
3. banana	nearest hundredth		nearest tenth	
4. ice	nearest hundredth		nearest ones	
5. milk	nearest hundredth		nearest tenth	
6. berries	nearest thousandth		nearest hundredth	
7. yogurt	nearest hundredth		nearest tenth	
8. protein powder	nearest thousandth		nearest ones	
9. oil	nearest ten-thousandth		nearest thousandth	

Name

SUM SPOKES

The tallest bicycle (that can be ridden) is **14.25** feet tall. If a rider's head and shoulders stand **1.09** feet above the handlebars, this makes the bicycle-rider combination **15.34** feet tall! In order to find this fact, you need to be able to add decimals.

Look, Ma, no hands!

The world's tallest bike looks something like this.

Practice decimal addition with the problems below. After you solve a problem, find the correct sum on the wheel.

Write the letter of the problem in the spoke with the matching sum.

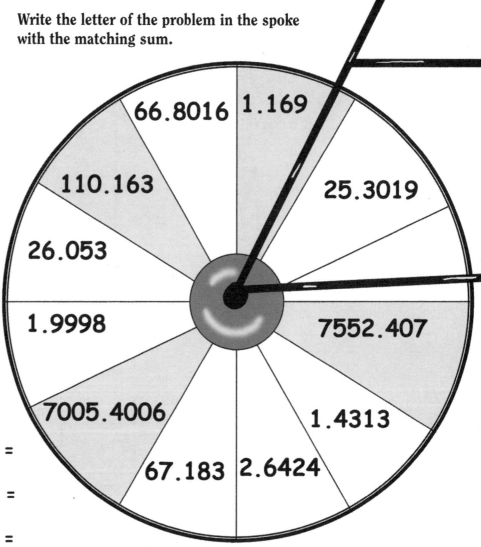

66.8016   1.169

110.163   25.3019

26.053

1.9998   7552.407

7005.4006   1.4313

67.183   2.6424

A. 2.4 + 0.2424 =

B. 4.06 + 21.993 =

C. 52.174 + 15.009 =

D. 7474.7 + 77.707 =

E. 0.9999 + 24.302 =

F. 3605.009 + 3400.3916 =

G. 0.1111 + 0.8888 + 0.9999 =

H. 22.211 + 22.59 + 22.0006 =

I. 0.1101 + 0.9909 + 0.3303 =

J. 1.088 + 0.0002 + 0.0808 =

K. 100.03 + 10.03 + 0.103 =

Name

DECIMALS ON WHEELS

Many sports demand skills with wheels. Use your own skills to solve these decimal problems about wheeled activities.

1. In 2003, Lance Armstrong won the Tour de France with an average speed of about 25.448 miles per hour. The 1995 winner, Miguel Indurain of Spain, had an average speed of 24.353 miles per hour. What was the difference in their speeds?

Answer_____

2. The first Tour de France was held in 1903. The winner was Maurice Garin of France. His average speed was 9.492 miles per hour slower than Armstrong's 2003 speed. (See problem 1.) What was Garin's speed?

Answer_____

3. Fastest un-paced women's 200-meter bicycle ride – **10.831 sec**
   Fastest un-paced men's 200-meter ride – **9.865 sec**   **The difference?** _____

4. Greatest distance bicycled in 24 hours – **1,958.196 km**
   Greatest distance bicycled in 1 hour – **49.44 km**   **The difference?** _____

5. Youngest Tour de France winner – **19.959 yrs**
   Oldest Tour de France winner – **16.378 yrs older**   **How old?** _____

6. Highest bunny hop on a mountain bike – **1.17 m**
   Longest standing jump on a mountain bike – **2.9 m**   **The difference?** _____

7. Highest ramp jump on a BMX bike – **5.12 m**
   Highest Moto X Step-Up Jump – **10.67 m**   **The difference?** _____

8. Farthest distance on in-line skates in 1 hour – **23.254 mi**
   Farthest distance on a unicycle in 1 hour – **6.617 mi less**   **How far?** _____

Name _____

DECIMAL WORKOUT

Get a workout of your skills by multiplying with decimals. Anya keeps this list of activities that are a part of her daily workout. Some of the numbers on her list will be needed for solving the problems.

Daily Workout

50	sit-ups
15	push-ups
0.75 hr	yoga
12.3 min	ball exercises
220	jump-rope skips
450	mini-trampoline bounces
0.5 hr	stretches

Grunt! Ooof!

_____ 1. The record for the most push-ups done in one minute was set at a rate of **2.2166** per second. Anna's rate is **0.17** times that rate. What is her rate? *(Round to nearest thousandth.)*

_____ 2. The record for the most sit-ups done in one minute was set at a rate of **2.3** per second. Anna's rate is **0.212** of that. What is her rate? *(Round to nearest thousandth.)*

_____ 3. Friend Kevin does yoga 3 times longer than Anna. How long?

_____ 4. She does the ball exercises 7 days in a row. How much total time?

_____ 5. Friday, she got in about 0.8 of her usual jump rope skips. How many?

_____ 6. She did 1.06 times the listed trampoline bounces today. How many?

_____ 7. Today she did 2.6 times the number of push-ups on her list. How many?

_____ 8. Her resting heart rate was 70. After exercise, it was 0.8 times faster. How fast?

_____ 9. She usually drinks 1.04 liters of water after jump-roping. Today she drank 2.3 times that much. How much?

_____ 10. Her exercise mat is 5.4 ft x 3.1 ft. What's the area?

Name _____

24

STEP UP TO DECIMALS

Step up to the task of multiplying decimals. When you find a solution, pay close attention to the locations of those decimal points in the products.

Finish the table below by calculating the times for Weeks 2–6.

C.J.'s Stair-Stepping Improvement

Which answer? Circle the correct letter.

Week	Minutes more than Week 1	Time On The Stepper (minutes)
1		40
2	1.05 times Week 1	
3	1.15 times Week 1	
4	1.25 times Week 1	
5	1.5 times Week 1	
6	1.6 times Week 1	

1. **12 x 15.5**
   a. 166.6
   b. 186
   c. 186.5

2. **0.4 x 0.04**
   a. 0.16
   b. 0.016
   c. 1.06

3. **33.7 x 4**
   a. 13.48
   b. 134.8
   c. 13.38
   d. none of these

4. **26.3 x 28**
   a. 734.4
   b. 73.64
   c. 736.4
   d. none of these

5. **660 x 1.75**
   a. 115.5
   b. 11.55
   c. 1155
   d. none of these

6. **466.8 x 3.91**
   a. 1825.188
   b. 18,231.88
   c. 182.5188
   d. none of these

7. **2.9 x 1.0572**
   a. 30.6588
   b. 3.06588
   c. 3.06468
   d. none of these

8. **75 x 100.23**
   a. 751.725
   b. 7407.15
   c. 75,170.5
   d. none of these

Name _____

DIVIDE AND CONQUER

Karate is a martial art that means "empty hand." This is because the athlete practices his art without any weapons. Karate is a mixture of punching and kicking techniques. One of the most popular and spectacular moves is the breaking of blocks of wood with the hands, feet, or head.

Use the facts in the "divided" blocks of wood to practice decimal division skills.

1 206.08 divided by 64

Answer_____

2 396 divided by 8.8

Answer_____

3 19.95 divided by 5.7

Answer_____

Ai...yeh!

4 113.22 divided by 2.04

Answer
_____

5 5.02853 divided by 0.611

Answer_____

6 0.5439 divided by 7.77

Answer_____

Name _____

MORE! Basic Skills/Decimals 6-8+

FOILED CALCULATIONS

A *foil* is a fencing sword with a flat guard for the hand and a thin blade with a blunt point. The blunt point allows the fighters to practice without getting injured.

The word *foil* also means to prevent from being successful.

Two math students, Tom and Amy, are taking a short test. They are competitive friends. Each one is making a lot of noise, trying to foil the other! The distractions are interfering with their work. Check both tests.

If the answer is wrong, write the correct answer near the problem number. Write *Yes* if the answer is correct.

Engarde!

Tom

1. $52\overline{)12.48}$ quotient 0.264

2. $3.5\overline{)427}$ quotient 112

3. $1.9\overline{)10.45}$ quotient 5.5

4. $5.2\overline{)57.2}$ quotient 1.1

5. $2.11\overline{)14.348}$ quotient 16.8

Tom

Amy

1. $43\overline{)15.05}$ quotient $.35$

2. $9.7\overline{)1125.2}$ quotient 11.6

3. $0.3\overline{)2.01}$ quotient 0.67

4. $7.8\overline{)257.4}$ quotient 23

5. $5.04\overline{)46.368}$ quotient 92

Amy

Name _____

MUSCLE POWER

The largest sumo wrestler on record weighed 227.249 kg. A sumo wrestler is a strong, powerful character.

Decimal numbers also become more powerful (they get larger) when they are multiplied by ten and multiples of ten.

Write the product on the blank line.

1. Axle A lifts **10.3** kg.   Bubba B lifts **10** times this.   _____

2. Chuck C lists **15.0166** kg.   Davy Doyle lifts **10** times this.   _____

3. Eddie Ernst lifts **2.62** kg.   Frankie Frank lifts **100** times this.   _____

4. Gus George lifts **0.052** kg.   Harry Hunk lifts **1,000** times this.   _____

5. Ken Kirk practices **1.092** hr.   Larry Lu practices **1,000** times this. _____

6. Moe Musser runs **2.066** mi.   Ned Nassy runs **10** times this.   _____

7. Pete Prune eats **113.955** calories. Quince Quick eats **10** times this.   _____

8. Ray Rumble travels **28.702** mi.   Sam Slick travels **1,000** times this. _____

9. **34.19 x 10,000 =**   _____

10. **0.007 x 1,000,000 =**   _____

11. **66.6666 x 100,000 =**   _____

12. **0.056632 x 100,000 =**   _____

Name _____

HEAVY LIFTING

The strongest heavy-lifter in the world is Hossein Rezazadeh from Iran. He holds the record for a "clean and jerk" lift of 263 kg. (That's 578.6 pounds—TEN times the weight that C.J. here can lift. You can divide 578.6 by 10 to find that C. J. lifts 57.86 pounds.)

Divide each set of numbers by the multiple of ten shown on the weights.

1. 40.03 _____

2. 92 _____

3. 617.526 _____

4. 1,272.15 _____

5. 36.1 _____

6. 4.5 _____

7. 0.55 _____

8. 2200.75 _____

9. 319,662 _____

10. 40,003.2 _____

11. 88,888 _____

12. 110,988.7 _____

13. 295.1 _____

14. 999 _____

15. 5 _____

16. 652,119.8 _____

17. 100 _____

18. 30,030 _____

Name _____

A WHITEWATER RACE

Race the rapids to the finish line by correctly solving each problem along the way.

1. Adam van Koeverden of Canada won the men's 500-meter K-1 (one person kayak) gold medal at the 2004 Olympics. His time was 1:37.919 (one minute, thirty-seven and nine hundred nineteen thousandths seconds). How many meters did he travel per second? *(Round to the nearest thousandth.)*

   Answer: _____

2. In 2000, Shaun Bader had a thrilling ride on a river in his home country (UK). He descended a vertical height of 75 feet in 19.9 seconds to break the record for fastest 75-ft descent by canoe. How many feet did he drop per second? *(Round to the nearest thousandth.)*

   Answer: _____

3. The men's 500-meter K-1 gold medal time was 1:37.919. The women's race was won in 1:47.741. What's the difference between the times?

   Answer: _____

4. Randy Fine (USA) holds the record for the most consecutive Eskimo rolls. He did 1,796. If another kayaker did 0.75 times that many, what would the second kayaker's number of rolls be?

   Answer: _____

5. Natasa Janics of Hungary won gold in the women's K-1 500-meter. Her winning time was 1:47.741. How many meters did she travel per second? *(Round to the nearest thousandth.)*

   Answer: _____

6. In 1987, kayaker Colin Hill (UK) did 1,000 Eskimo rolls in 31 min, 55 sec. What was his rate of rolls per second? *(Round to the nearest thousandth.)*

   Answer: _____

7. Two paddlers from France rolled 23 times in one minute. How long did each roll take? *(Round to the nearest thousandth.)*

   Answer: _____

Name _____

IT TAKES A CREW

The sport of rowing takes strength and discipline. Rowers sit in a scull (boat) and row in singles or crews of 2, 4, or 8. One of the fastest rowing records was set in 1999 by a crew of 8 from the Netherlands. They completed the 2,000-meter course in 5:22.80 (five minutes, twenty-two and eight tenths seconds.)

Answers

1. The women's record for quadruple sculls was set by a German crew in 1996. They covered a 2000-meter course in 6:10.80. What is the per-second rate of their race? (Round to the nearest thousandths.) _____

2. The men's quadruple sculls record was set in 1994 by a team from Italy. They covered the 2000-meter distance in 5:37.68 minutes. How fast did they travel per second? _____

3. What was the difference in the women's and men's times (problems 1 and 2)? _____

4. In a race of lightweight sculls, four women from Australia won the race with a time of 6:29.55. What is the difference between this time and the winning time of the regular quadruple scull race (problem 1)? _____
   Do the lightweight sculls move faster or slower than the regular sculls? _____

5. The average weight of four crewmembers is 158.75 pounds. Here are the weights of three of them: 138.5 pounds, 174.2 pounds, 166.8 pounds. What is the weight of the fourth crewmember? _____

6. The greatest single scull record was set by Roumiana Neykova, from Bulgaria. His time was 7:7.71. Another rower finished the course in 8:12.89. How much faster was Neykova's time? _____

7. One rower practices by rowing 10,000 meters on Monday. On Tuesday, he rows 0.05 times more distance than Monday. On Wednesday, he rows 0.05 times more distance than on Tuesday. How far does he row on Wednesday? _____

Name _____

DECIMALS TAKE A DIVE

Free diving is a sport that keeps an athlete underwater for a long time—without help from any breathing devices! A diver descends as far as possible underwater—while holding his or her breath. Divers might dive as deep as 600 feet, and stay underwater for up to 8 minutes.

1 A diver descends 550.3 feet below the surface. Then she heads upwards for a distance of 60.5 feet. What is her location now in relation to the surface? You can find out by solving this problem:
550.3 – (-60.5 ft) =_____

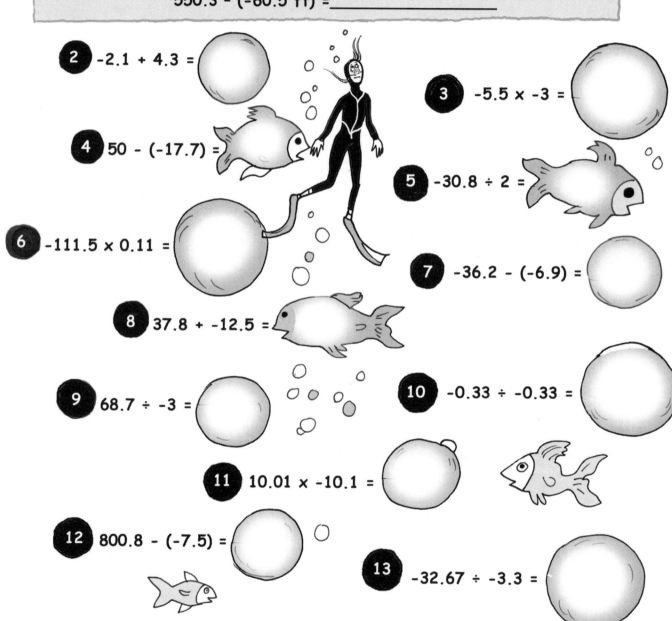

2 -2.1 + 4.3 =

3 -5.5 x -3 =

4 50 - (-17.7) =

5 -30.8 ÷ 2 =

6 -111.5 x 0.11 =

7 -36.2 - (-6.9) =

8 37.8 + -12.5 =

9 68.7 ÷ -3 =

10 -0.33 ÷ -0.33 =

11 10.01 x -10.1 =

12 800.8 - (-7.5) =

13 -32.67 ÷ -3.3 =

Name

SPRINGBOARD SOLUTIONS

Greg Louganis (USA) won five world titles and four Olympic gold medals. That's a lot of diving! His total points in springboard diving in the 1988 Olympic games was 754.41. The 1980 winner, Aleksandr Portnov (USSR), had a score of 905.02. To compare the scores, it could be said that Louganis had a score of –150.61.

1. Only two Olympic divers have won a total of 5 medals. Another diver won 0.6 times as many. How many did the third diver win?

   Problem: _____

   Answer: _____

2. A diver headed off the board and dove into the water, ending 10.9 feet below the surface (–10.9). She traveled a total of 26.7 feet from her highest point in the air. How high above the surface was she when she began the dive?

   Problem: _____

   Answer: _____

3. On Alex's first dive, he plunged to 3.6 feet below the surface. On the second dive, the plunge was 0.5 the distance. Where, in relation to the surface of the water, did this second dive leave him?

   Problem: _____

   Answer: _____

4. Diver Emma had a roll of 95.35 ft of athletic tape. She gave equal amounts of the tape to five friends, using up the whole roll. How much tape (length) did each friend get?

   Problem: _____

   Answer: _____

Write a number sentence to solve each problem. Then find the solution.

5. Marika dove 8.6 feet below the surface. From there, she descended another 1.9 ft. What was her position then in relation to the water's surface?

   Problem: _____

   Answer: _____

6. A diver dove 11.4 feet below the surface. He rose 3.7 feet. Where was he then in relation to the water's surface?

   Problem: _____

   Answer: _____

Name _____

THE SHORT WAY TO SAY IT

Beach volleyball is played out in the sand under the sun. Even though the distance from Earth to the sun is 93,000,000 miles, the summer games can be hot!

Scientific notation provides a short way to write this distance: **9.3×10^7**. Brush up on the right way to write big numbers with scientific notation.

Use scientific notation to rewrite the number in each example. Write the short way on the line.

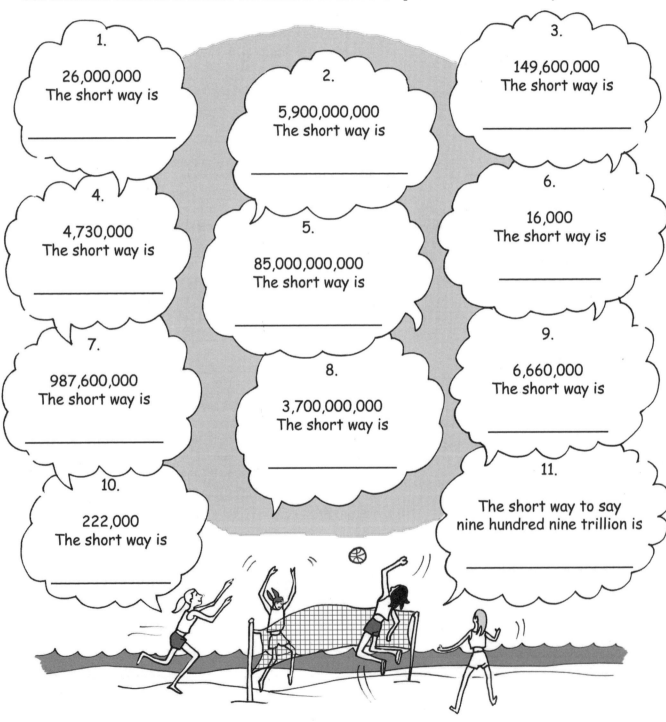

1.
26,000,000
The short way is
_____

2.
5,900,000,000
The short way is
_____

3.
149,600,000
The short way is
_____

4.
4,730,000
The short way is
_____

5.
85,000,000,000
The short way is
_____

6.
16,000
The short way is
_____

7.
987,600,000
The short way is
_____

8.
3,700,000,000
The short way is
_____

9.
6,660,000
The short way is
_____

10.
222,000
The short way is
_____

11.
The short way to say
nine hundred nine trillion is
_____

Name _____

SAILING THROUGH BIG NUMBERS

The fastest round-the-world sailing journey in an 88-foot yacht took 72 days, 22 hours, 54 minutes, and 22 seconds. This is about **1.05×10^5** hours (written in scientific notation). In ordinary notation, this is 105,000 hours of traveling on the water!

Read these other numbers in scientific notation. On the body of each boat, write the regular notation for the number shown on the sail.

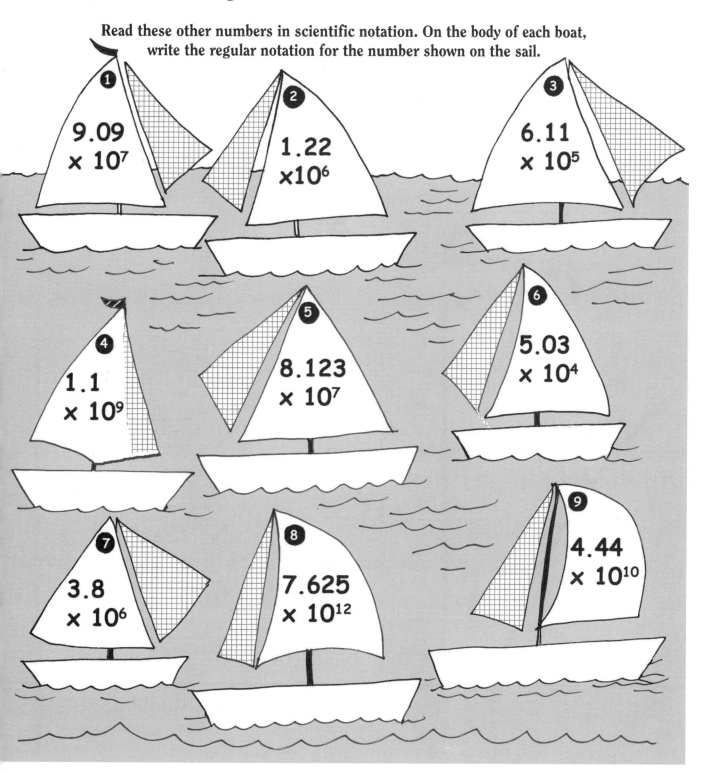

1. 9.09×10^7

2. 1.22×10^6

3. 6.11×10^5

4. 1.1×10^9

5. 8.123×10^7

6. 5.03×10^4

7. 3.8×10^6

8. 7.625×10^{12}

9. 4.44×10^{10}

Name

HIGH-FLYING MOVES

In the pole vault, athletes soar into the air on a flexible pole. The goal is to cross a high bar without knocking it down. Pole-vaulters need plenty of practice, because the bar is raised higher and higher.

Write each fraction below as a decimal numeral (rounded to the nearest thousandth).

The bar will get higher as you get farther into the exercise, because the problems get harder.

A. Yelena Isinbayeva, from Russia, set the women's world pole vault record in 2003. She cleared a bar that was $4\frac{1}{50}$ meters high.

Write the fraction as a decimal. _____

B. Sergei Bubka, from Ukraine, set the men's world pole vault record in 1994. He cleared a bar that was $6\frac{7}{50}$ meters high.

Write the fraction as a decimal. _____

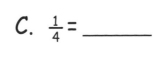

C. $\frac{1}{4} =$ _____

D. $\frac{4}{5} =$ _____

E. $25\frac{3}{4} =$ _____

F. $\frac{2}{5} =$ _____

G. $\frac{5}{8} =$ _____

H. $10\frac{3}{5} =$ _____

I. $\frac{7}{16} =$ _____

J. $\frac{2}{3} =$ _____

K. $\frac{11}{12} =$ _____

L. $\frac{5}{9} =$ _____

M. $4\frac{5}{6} =$ _____

N. $10\frac{2}{3} =$ _____

O. $25\frac{5}{7} =$ _____

P. $4\frac{7}{8} =$ _____

Q. $25\frac{7}{9} =$ _____

Name _____

HIGH-POWERED THROWS

Four sports in the track and field category involve throwing things. Athletes throw a javelin (a spear-like pole), a shot (a solid metal ball), a discus (a smooth metal and wood circular "plate"), or a hammer (a metal sphere attached to a handle by a thin metal wire). The hammer is a men's sport only. All these throws take power, balance, and skill.

Write a fraction to replace each decimal. Then solve the puzzle below.

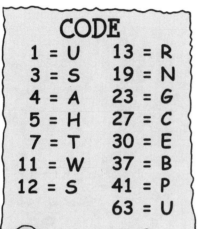

CODE

1 = U	13 = R
3 = S	19 = N
4 = A	23 = G
5 = H	27 = C
7 = T	30 = E
11 = W	37 = B
12 = S	41 = P
	63 = U

1. Women's javelin record is **71.54** meters, or _____

2. Men's shot put record is **23.12** meters, or _____

3. Women's shot put record is **22.63** meters, or _____

4. Women's discus record is **76.8** meters, or _____

5. Men's discus record is **74.08** meters, or _____

6. Men's hammer record is **86.74** meters, or _____

7. Men's javelin record is **98.48** meters, or _____

8. Women's shot weighs about **8.8** pounds, or _____

9. Minimum weight of a hammer is **7.26** kilograms, or _____

10. Minimum diameter of a shot is **3.75** inches, or _____

11. The diameter of the circle in which the discus event takes place is **2.5** meters, or _____

What are the countries of the record-holders in problems 1, 2, and 3?

Look at the problem number beneath each line. Find the numerator of the fraction in the answer to that problem. Find that numerator on the Code List. Write the matching letter into the puzzle to find the names of the countries.

____ ____ ____ ____ , ____ ____ ____ , ____ ____ ____ ____

#1   #3   #6   #8   #5   #2   #4   #11   #10   #7   #9

Name _____

SOME FANCY SWIMMING

Synchronized swimming is an amazing sport to watch. Swimmers coordinate their movements to create complicated figures and exciting routines in the water.

At one synchronized swimming competition, ten teams competed. A total of 1,680 fans watched the competition. The fraction or decimal values were found by dividing the number of fans for each team by the total number of fans (1,680). Fill in the table with the missing decimal or percentage values.

Name of Team	# of fans	Fraction or Decimal Value	Percentage
A. In-Sync	180	0.107	_____
B. Tampa Tempo	93	_____	5.5%
C. Wave Breakers	116	0.069	_____
D. Silver Splash	158	0.094	_____
E. Fantastic Floaters	252	$\frac{3}{20}$	_____
F. Southern Ladies	148	_____	8.8%
G. Sub-Splendor	162	0.096	_____
H. Awesome Eight	294	_____	17.5%
I. Aqua Velvet	67	_____	4%
J. Sync-Sisters	210	$\frac{1}{8}$	_____

This table gives data about the number of participants at a competition. The percent of change in numbers is shown for each region. Fill in the table with the missing percentage or decimal values.

Region	2004	2005	% change	Decimal Value
1. East	40	48	20%	_____
2. South	32	64	_____	2.0
3. Great Lakes	72	8	_____	0.111
4. Midwest	80	72	10%	_____
5. Southwest	64	24	267%	_____
6. Rocky Mts	48	56	_____	0.166
7. Pacific Coast	120	104	13.3%	_____

Name _____

WAITING FOR THE WAVES

During surfing practice and competitions, a lot of time is spent waiting for the right wave. Surfer Sam has passed up 22 of the last 25 waves. This is **88%** of the waves. Written as a decimal, this is **0.88**.

Find the decimals and percents tossed in the surf.

If the number is in decimal form, re-write it as a percent. If the number is expressed as a percent, re-write it as a decimal numeral.

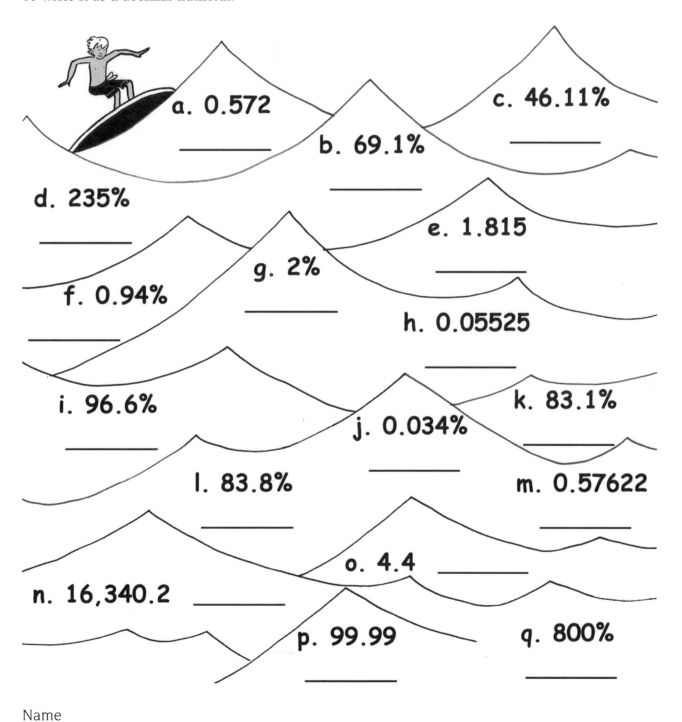

a. 0.572

b. 69.1%

c. 46.11%

d. 235%

e. 1.815

f. 0.94%

g. 2%

h. 0.05525

i. 96.6%

j. 0.034%

k. 83.1%

l. 83.8%

m. 0.57622

n. 16,340.2

o. 4.4

p. 99.99

q. 800%

Name

ON TARGET

In many competitions, archers add up a score after six arrows. Add up the scores of these arrows. This total will become a fact needed to calculate some percentages.

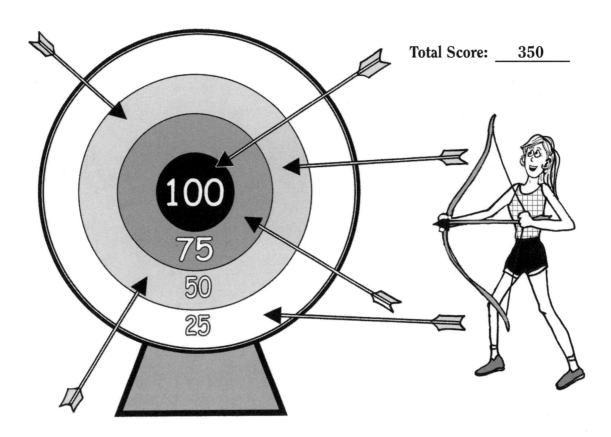

Total Score: ___350___

Round answers to the nearest tenth.

1. Percent of arrows scoring 75? _____

2. Percent of the arrows scoring 50? _____

3. Percent of the arrows scoring 100? _____

4. Percent of the total score from 50s? _____

5. Ring accounting for 21.4% of score? _____

6. Ring accounting for 28.6% of score? _____

7. Ring accounting for 7.141% of score? _____

8. What is 55% of 820? _____

9. 65 is 22% of 450—yes or no? _____

10. What is 48% of 400? _____

11. 30.38 is 62% of 49—yes or no? _____

12. What is 17% of 828? _____

Name

BULL'S-EYE PERCENTAGES

Find the answers to these percentage problems on the targets below.

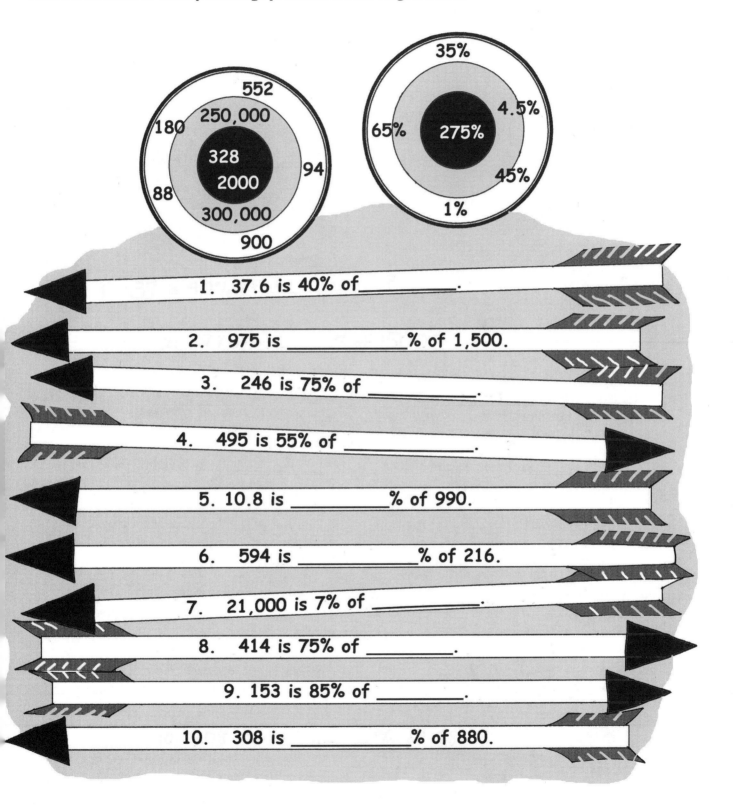

1. 37.6 is 40% of _____.

2. 975 is _____ % of 1,500.

3. 246 is 75% of _____.

4. 495 is 55% of _____.

5. 10.8 is _____ % of 990.

6. 594 is _____ % of 216.

7. 21,000 is 7% of _____.

8. 414 is 75% of _____.

9. 153 is 85% of _____.

10. 308 is _____ % of 880.

Name _____

IT TAKES A CROWD

Crowds are an important part of sporting events. The fans add to the excitement of any game or competition. It takes a crowd of people to run big sporting events and keep them safe. Sometimes, the game or competition itself involves a crowd of participants!

_____ 1. About 300 athletes participated in the first modern Olympic Games. The 2004 Summer Olympics in Athens hosted 10,500 athletes. What is the percent of change in the number of participants?

_____ 2. The number of countries represented at the 2004 Summer Olympics was about 200. This represented a 1,438.5% change over the number in the 1896 Olympics. Which number is probably the number of countries participating in 1896?

    a. 28   b. 13   c. 130   d. 71

_____ 3. 11,084 athletes participated in the 2000 Sydney Olympics. Of these, 4,245 were women. What percent of the athletes were men?

_____ 4. 5,797,923 people attended the 1984 Los Angeles Summer Olympics. If about 35% were visitors from outside the USA, about how many people were USA residents?

_____ 5. The largest circle dance on record involved 6,748 people. Assume that 5,061 of these participants had never danced before. What percent would that be?

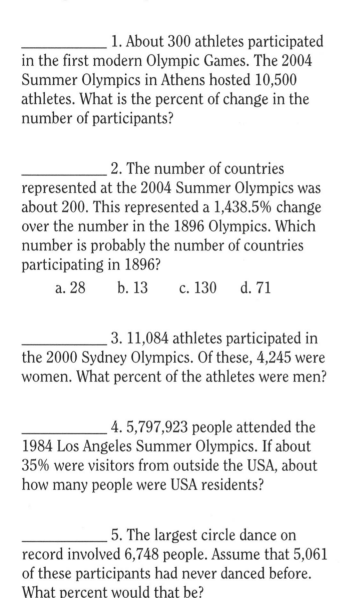

I think I'm being paintball slimed!

_____ 6. In 2002, 6,900,000 people played paintball! This was a 24.4% change in numbers from the previous year. About how many people participated in 2001?

    a. 5,546,600   b. 6,135,800   c. 5,175.000

_____ 7. At the 2004 Summer Olympics in Athens, about 45,000 people had jobs related to security. These included police, military personnel, and volunteers. If 55% were volunteers, how many were police or military personnel?

_____ 8. 931 gold medals have been given in Olympic games from 1896 to 2000. In the 2000 games, the USA women's 4 x 200 meter freestyle swim team won 4 of those gold medals. What percent of the total medals did they win?

_____ 9. In April of 2003, at a school in the UK, 1,356 children skipped rope at the same time. If 50% of them were over 10 years old, how many would be under 10?

Name _____

ARENA STATISTICS

Fans fill arenas for sporting events. Use your skills in finding percentages to solve these problems about some things that go on in the arena.

1. The largest sports arena in the world (not counting horse racetracks or motor racetracks) is the Strahov Stadium in Prague. It holds 250,000 spectators. If a game began with every seat filled, but 65% of the people left during a rainstorm, about how many spectators would remain?

    Answer: _____

2. The largest soccer stadium in the world is in Rio de Janeiro, Brazil. It holds 205,000 people. Only 155,000 of these spectators can be seated. What percentage must stand?

    Answer: _____

3. Fans in arena: 30,800
   Percent wearing team colors: 80%

   How many in team colors? _____

4. Fans in arena: 200,000
   Percent standing: 48%

   How many sitting? _____

5. Fans in arena: 54,000
   Number with umbrellas: 31,320

   Percent with umbrellas? _____

6. Fans in arena: 122,500
   Percent eating hot dogs: 85%

   How many eating hot dogs? _____

7. Fans in arena: 4,780
   Number in box seats: 717

   Percent in box seats? _____

8. Fans in arena: 97,200
   Number with hoarse voices: 66,096

   Percent with hoarse voices? _____

Name _____

FEED THE TEAM

All that activity has the baseball team members hungry. Figure out how much each one will spend. Don't forget the tax and the tip.

MENU

spaghetti......................$7.90
pizza.............................$12.50
lasagna.........................$13.50
tacos.............................$2.50 ea
enchilada plate............$6.25
steak and salad............$16.35
hamburger & fries........$9.95
milkshake......................$4.00
all other drinks............$1.50
pie.................................$3.50

Add 6% tax. Figure the 15% tip on the subtotal before tax is added.

Brad

Spaghetti	___
2 Tacos	___
Drink	___
Pie	___
Subtotal	___
+ Tip	___
+ Tax	___
Total	___

Fred

Burger & Fries	___
Steak & Salad	___
Milkshake	___
Subtotal	___
+ Tip	___
+ Tax	___
Total	___

Ted

Steak & Salad	___
Enchilada Plate	___
Milkshake	___
Pie	___
Subtotal	___
+ Tip	___
+ Tax	___
Total	___

Tad

2 Burgers & Fries	___
2 Tacos	___
Milkshake	___
Pie	___
Subtotal	___
+ Tip	___
+ Tax	___
Total	___

Chad

Lasagna	___
Pizza	___
Milkshake	___
Pie	___
Subtotal	___
+ Tip	___
+ Tax	___
Total	___

Name _____

QUESTIONS OF INTEREST

Interest is a sum of money that a buyer pays for the privilege of using someone else's money for a while. (That someone else is a bank, credit card company, or other lender.)

Find the missing figures for simple interest, original loan amount, loan time, principal, or total due. Look for, and fill in, blank spaces.

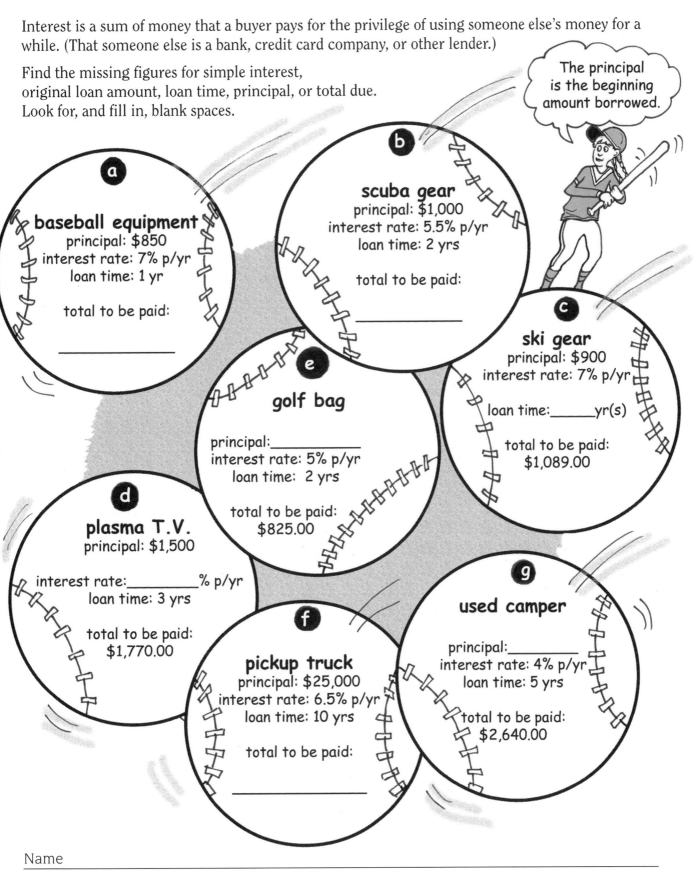

The principal is the beginning amount borrowed.

a
baseball equipment
principal: $850
interest rate: 7% p/yr
loan time: 1 yr

total to be paid:
_____

b
scuba gear
principal: $1,000
interest rate: 5.5% p/yr
loan time: 2 yrs

total to be paid:
_____

c
ski gear
principal: $900
interest rate: 7% p/yr

loan time: _____ yr(s)

total to be paid:
$1,089.00

e
golf bag

principal: _____
interest rate: 5% p/yr
loan time: 2 yrs

total to be paid:
$825.00

d
plasma T.V.
principal: $1,500

interest rate: _____% p/yr
loan time: 3 yrs

total to be paid:
$1,770.00

f
pickup truck
principal: $25,000
interest rate: 6.5% p/yr
loan time: 10 yrs

total to be paid:
_____

g
used camper

principal: _____
interest rate: 4% p/yr
loan time: 5 yrs

total to be paid:
$2,640.00

Name

MORE! Basic Skills/Decimals 6-8+

HOT TICKETS

Find the prices of the tickets for these various groups of spectators. Watch the decimal point carefully as you operate with money. Round any amounts of money to the nearest whole cent.

Ticket Prices

adults..........................$21.00
children (5-12)...........$15.50
children (3-4)..............$4.25
children (0-2)..............free
seniors (over 65).......$16.00

groups of more than 35
20% discount

1. McCall family: 6 adults, 2 seniors

   Cost: _____

2. Adams family: child (age 3), child (age 9), 1 adult parent, 1 senior.
   Nelson family: 3 times the cost of the Adams family.

   Cost for Nelsons: _____

3. Group of 37 adults.
   Group of 46 adults.

   Difference in cost: _____

4. Church group; 20 children (age 11), 10 adults
   Community group: 1/5 the cost

   Community group cost: _____

5. Child (age 2), child (age 6), child (age 1), child (age 10), 3 adults, 2 seniors

   Cost: _____

6. School group: 135 children (ages 6–10)

   Cost: _____

7. High school group: 268 teenagers

   Total savings due to discount: _____

Name

TOP DOLLARS

Many professional athletes earn huge salaries. Use your decimal skills to solve these problems about top dollars in sports.

_____ 1. Tennis player Serena Williams is the highest-earning female athlete. In 2004 she earned $9,500,000. What would be the earnings of a player who earned 35% as much?

_____ 2. Tiger Woods has the highest career earnings on the U.S. Professional Golf Association circuit. He won $41,508,265 from August, 1996 to March, 2004. If he gave away 30% of his earnings, how much would that be?

_____ 3. By the end of the 2003 season, tennis player Steffi Graf had earned $21,895,277 in her career. How much less is that than Tiger Woods earned up to March, 2004? (See problem 2.)

_____ 4. A bodybuilder, Arnold Schwarzenegger, earned $30,000,000 for his 2001 role in a movie, **Terminator 3**. If the film took 25 days to film, how much would he earn per day?

_____ 5. Karch Kiraly, beach volleyball player, had accumulated $2,844,065 by August, 2000. If he earned half again that much in the rest of his career, what would his total earnings be?

_____ 6. A high-earning surfer, Kelly Slater, had earned $708,230 by 1998. What would he have left if he paid 35% in taxes?

_____ 7. Even though he is retired, Michael Jordan earned about $35,000,000 in endorsements in 2004. How much more is this than Kelly Slater's career earnings? (See problem 6.)

_____ 8. In 2004, racecar driver Michael Schumacher earned $80,000,000. This was about $300,000 less than golfer Tiger Woods, making him the second highest earning athlete of the year. How much did Tiger earn that year?

_____ 9. Alex Rodriguez earned $26,400,000 playing baseball in 2004. He has been promised $252,000,000 over 10 years. What will Rodriguez's average yearly salary be over 10 years?

_____ 10. Football player Peyton Manning got the largest signing bonus ever. When he agreed to play for a team in the NFL, he was promised $34,500,000. How much more is this than Alex Rodriguez's 2004 salary? (See problem 9.)

Name _____

REPEAT THAT!

It is very difficult to get a hole-in-one in golf. Imagine how hard it must be to repeat the feat! Twenty times, someone has gotten a hole-in-one, said, "Now I'll repeat that," and did! Norman L. Manley of Saugus, California is responsible for one of the best repeats (1964).

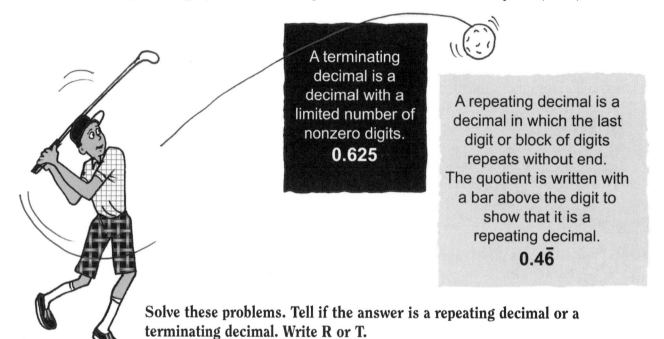

A terminating decimal is a decimal with a limited number of nonzero digits.
0.625

A repeating decimal is a decimal in which the last digit or block of digits repeats without end. The quotient is written with a bar above the digit to show that it is a repeating decimal.
0.4$\overline{6}$

Solve these problems. Tell if the answer is a repeating decimal or a terminating decimal. Write R or T.

_____ 1. A golfer got a hole-in-one in three different games of the 4,017 games of golf he played. What percent of games did he play in which he did NOT get a hole-in-one?

_____ 2. A golfer earned $100,000 in her fifth year as a professional golfer. The following year, she earned one-third that much. How much were her sixth year earnings?

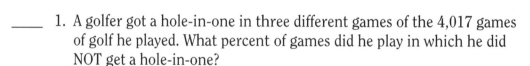

Rename these fractions as decimals. Write R or T to describe the decimals.

R/T		Decimal	R/T		Decimal
_____	3. $\frac{3}{16}$ =	_____	_____	8. $\frac{5}{16}$ =	_____
_____	4. $\frac{1}{15}$ =	_____	_____	9. $\frac{7}{25}$ =	_____
_____	5. $\frac{2}{9}$ =	_____	_____	10. $\frac{12}{25}$ =	_____
_____	6. $\frac{2}{5}$ =	_____	_____	11. $\frac{5}{6}$ =	_____
_____	7. $\frac{9}{20}$ =	_____	_____	12. $\frac{5}{8}$ =	_____

Name _____

Appendix

Contents

GLOSSARY OF DECIMAL TERMS

associative property – a property of addition or multiplication stating that changing the grouping of numbers does not change the sum or product

Example: 3.2 + (0.4 + 1.1) = (3.2 + 0.4) + 1.1

commutative property – a property of addition or multiplication stating that changing the order of numbers does not change the sum or product

Example: 5.1 + 9.2 = 9.2 + 5.1
8 x 4.5 = 4.5 x 8

cross multiplication – a process for solving proportions where the numerator of one fraction is multiplied with the denominator of a second fraction. That product is compared with the product that comes from multiplying the denominator of the first fraction with the numerator of the second.

decimal numeral – name for a fractional number expressed with a decimal point

Example: 0.37 (meaning 37 hundredths) is a decimal numeral; 5.37 is a mixed decimal numeral

decimal system – a numeration system based on grouping by tens

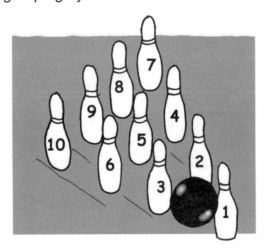

denominator – the bottom number in a fraction

Example: 10.5 is the denominator in the fraction $\frac{5}{10.5}$

divisible – capable of being divided evenly without a remainder

Example: 21.3 is divisible by 0.3

equation – a number sentence which states that two numbers or quantities are equal

Example: 35.9 + x = 136.2

estimate – an answer that is not exact, but is close to the actual answer

fraction – a number that compares part of an object or set to the whole object or set; this number appears in the form of $\frac{a}{b}$, where b is not zero

identity property for addition – property stating that the sum of 0 and any number is that number

Example: 10.2 + 0 = 10.2

identity property for multiplication – property stating that the product of 1 and any number is that number

Example: 9.999 x 1 = 9.999

inequality – a number sentence that states two numbers or quantities are not equal

Example: 6.5 + 3 > 2.5 + 4

integers – the set of numbers that includes the positive numbers 1, 2, 3, …, the negative numbers, –1, –2, –3, …, and zero.

interest – money that is paid for the use of money

interest rate – a percent used to calculate interest

irrational number – any real number that cannot be expressed as the exact ratio of two integers. It is expressed as a non-terminating, non-repeating decimal.

loan period – the period of time over which money is loaned and interest accumulates

mixed number – a number that has a whole number part and a fractional number part. Mixed numbers can be mixed fractions or mixed decimals.

mixed decimal number – a number that has a whole number part and a decimal part
Example: 85.39

multiple – the product of a given number and any whole number
Example: 2.6, 3.9, 5.2, and 6.5 are all multiples of 1.3

number sentence – a sentence showing a relationship among numbers
Example: 85.7 = 44.3 + 41.4

numerator – the top number in a fraction
Example: 5.5 is the numerator in the fraction $\frac{5.5}{20}$

percent – the ratio of a number to 100, expressed using the % symbol
Example: 56.5% is a comparison of 56.5 to 100

percentage – a part of a total amount

principal – the money deposited, borrowed, or loaned, on which interest accumulates

product – the answer in a multiplication problem
Example: In 4 x 3.5 = 14, the product is 14

proportion – an equation which states that two ratios are equal
Example: $\frac{8}{10} = \frac{4}{5}$

We're equal, you know!

rate – a ratio that compares quantities of two different kinds. A rate may be expressed as a percent, a decimal, or a ratio.

ratio – the quotient of two numbers that is used to compare one quantity to another
Example: The distance (6.5 miles) someone runs in an hour (60 min) might be expressed as a ratio ($\frac{6.5}{60}$)

rational number – any number that can be written as the quotient of two integers $\frac{a}{b}$, where b is not zero. Also all terminating and repeating decimals

repeating decimal – a decimal in which the last digit or block of digits repeats without end
Example: 3.333333 . . . (written $3.\overline{3}$)

tax – a percentage of an earning or purchase calculated with a decimal amount

terminating decimal – a decimal with a limited number of nonzero digits
Example: 0.526

MORE! Basic Skills/Decimals 6-8+   51

Handbook of Decimal Skills

Decimals

A **decimal** is a way of writing a fractional number that has a denominator of 10 or a multiple of 10.

Decimals are written using a decimal point. The decimal point is placed to the right of the ones place.

$$1 = 1.0$$
$$\frac{1}{10} = .1$$
$$\frac{1}{100} = .01$$
$$\frac{1}{1,000} = .001$$
$$\frac{1}{10,000} = .0001$$

Terminating Decimals

A **terminating decimal** is a decimal number that ends. When a quotient for a divided fraction eventually shows a remainder of zero, the decimal terminates.

When $\frac{5}{8}$ is divided, the result is a terminating decimal:

0.625

Repeating Decimals

A **repeating decimal** is a decimal that has one or more digits that repeat indefinitely. The quotient for a divided fraction never results in a remainder of zero, and one or more of the final digits keep repeating. A repeating decimal is indicated by a bar written above the numbers that repeat.

When $\frac{1}{3}$ is divided, the result is a repeating decimal: **0.3$\overline{3}$**

Place Value in Decimals

Places to the right of the ones place show decimals.
A decimal point separates the ones place from the tenths place.

The chart below shows six places to the right of the decimal point.

Number	tens	ones	tenths	hundredths	thousandths	ten thousandths	hundred thousandths	millionths
5.5		5.	5					
1.123		1.	1	2	3			
.0071		0.	0	0	7	1		
.15055		0.	1	5	0	5	5	
12.000866	1	2.	0	0	0	8	6	6

Reading & Writing Decimals

Read the whole number first. Then read the entire number to the right of the decimal point, adding the label from the place of the last digit.

Mixed decimal numbers combine whole numbers and decimals. A mixed number has digits on both sides of the decimal point.

5.5	reads	*five and five tenths*
1.123	reads	*one and one hundred twenty-three thousandths*
0.0071	reads	*seventy-one ten thousandths*
0.15055	reads	*fifteen thousand fifty-five hundred thousandths*
12.000866	reads	*twelve and eight hundred sixty-six millionths*

Rounding Decimals

Decimals are rounded in the same way as whole numbers.
If a digit is 5 or greater, round up to the next highest number in the place to the left.
If the digit is 4 or less, round down.

0.005	*rounded to the nearest hundred is*	**0.01**
0.63	*rounded to the nearest tenth is*	**0.6**
5.068	*rounded to the nearest tenth is*	**5.1**
5.068	*rounded to the nearest hundredth is*	**5.07**

$10.8333

rounds to

$10.83

Adding & Subtracting Decimals

Step 1: Line up the decimal point in both numbers in the problem.

Step 2: Add or subtract just as with whole numbers.

Step 3: Align the decimal point in the sum or difference with decimal points in the numbers above.

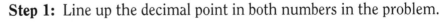

12.60

0.70

+

13.30   -   10.25   -   3.05   =   0

Multiplying Decimals

Step 1: Multiply as you would with whole numbers.

Step 2: Count the number of places to the right of the decimal point in both factors (the total of the places in the two numbers).

Step 3: Count over from the right end of the product that same number of places.

Step 4: Insert the decimal point.

Dividing Decimals

Step 1: When the divisor is a decimal, count the number of places you must move the decimal point to the right to make the divisor a whole number.

Step 2: Move the decimal point in the dividend the same number of places to the right.

Step 3: Divide as you would with whole numbers.

Step 4: Add zeros where necessary to hold places.

Step 5: Align the decimal point in the quotient with the decimal point in the dividend.

To Write a Fraction as a Decimal

Step 1: Divide the numerator by the denominator.

Step 2: Write a zero to hold the ones place (if there is no number in that place).

$$\frac{7}{25} = 0.28$$

To Write a Decimal as a Fraction

Step 1: Remove the decimal point and write the number as the numerator. The denominator is 10 or a multiple of 10, depending on what place the last digit of the decimal occupies. (For instance, in **0.355**, the last digit is a thousandth, so the denominator is 1000.)

Step 2: Reduce the fraction to lowest terms.

$0.3 = 3 \text{ tenths} = \frac{3}{10}$

$0.24 = 24 \text{ hundredths} = \frac{24}{100} = \frac{6}{25}$

$5.75 = 5 \text{ and } 75 \text{ hundredths} = 5\frac{75}{100} = 5\frac{3}{4}$

To Write a Decimal as a Percent

Move the decimal point **two places to the right.**

$0.465 = 46.5\%$

$15.4 = 1540\%$

To Write a Percent as a Decimal

Move the decimal point **two places to the left.**

$19.6\% = 0.196$

$124\% = 12.4$

To Write a Fraction as a Percent

Divide the numerator by the denominator.

Then move the decimal point **two places to the right.**

$$\frac{3}{10} = 3 \div 10 = 0.30 = 30\%$$

$$\frac{4}{5} = 4 \div 5 = 0.80 = 80\%$$

Tip
Remember this:
Decimal to Percent—
move right!
Percent to Decimal—
move left!

To Find a Percentage of a Number

Percentage is a part of a total amount.

To find a percentage of a number:

Step 1: Change the percent to a decimal.

Step 2: Multiply the number by that decimal.

What is 15% of 200?

Step 1: 15% = 0.15

Step 2: 0.15 × 200 =
30.00 = 30

To Tell What Percent One Number is of Another

To tell what percent one number is of a second number:

Step 1: Divide the first number by the second.

Step 2: Move the decimal point of the quotient two places to the right.

24 is what % of 96?

Step 1: 24 ÷ 96 = 0.25

Step 2: 0.25 = 25%

To Find the Base When You Know the Percent

When you know the percent and the resulting percentage (part of the total number) but not the base number (the original number):

Step 1: Change the percent to a decimal.

Step 2: Divide the percentage number by that decimal.

112 is 80% of what?

Step 1: 80% = 0.80

Step 2: 112 ÷ 0.8 = 140

DECIMALS SKILLS TEST

Questions 1–75: worth 1 point each
Problems 76–80: worth 5 points each

1–5: Match the decimal numerals to the words.
Write the correct letter.

____ 1. two and two thousandths

____ 2. two hundred two ten-thousandths

____ 3. two and two hundredths

____ 4. two and two tenths

____ 5. twenty-two hundredths

A. 22.02	F. 0.02
B. 2.002	G. 2.02
C. 0.022	H. 0.0202
D. 2.202	I. 0.20
E. 2.2	J. 0.22

6–11: Write the decimal numeral.

_____ 6. five and five hundredths

_____ 7. fifty-five and five tenths

_____ 8. two and six thousandths

_____ 9. sixty-three thousandths

_____ 10. eighty-nine hundredths

_____ 11. fourteen hundred-thousandths

12–14: Write the words to match the numeral.

12. Write the words: **0.00007** _____

13. Write the words: **0.104** _____

14. Write the words: **17.03** _____

15–20: Tell the place value of the bold digit.

_____ 15. 3.567**8**

_____ 16. **0**.259

_____ 17. 13.6**5**2

_____ 18. 0.0000**4**

_____ 19. **2**5.699

_____ 20. 0.9**2**8

Name _____

MORE! Basic Skills/Decimals 6-8+

21–25: *Round the number from the T-shirt to the nearest place as directed in each problem.*

_____ 21. tenths

_____ 22. thousandths

_____ 23. tens

_____ 24. hundredths

_____ 25. ones

75.3694

26–29: *Compare these decimals. Write* **<**, **>**, *or* **=** *in each blank.*

26. 6.5061 _____ 6.5106   28. 26.05 _____ 26.050

27. 0.111 _____ 0.099   29. 0.1504 _____ 0.1450

30. Put these decimals in order from smallest to largest.

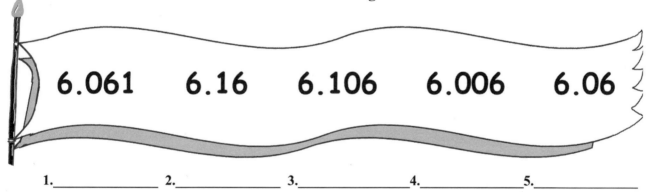

6.061   6.16   6.106   6.006   6.06

1._____ 2._____ 3._____ 4._____ 5._____

31–40: *Solve these problems. Round decimal answers to the nearest hundred-thousandth.*

31. 12 x 15.5 = _____   36. 95.36 ÷ 100 = _____

32. 6.2 + 0.035 – 2.9 = _____   37. 0.4292 x 10,000 = _____

33. –45.3 – (–10.2) = _____   38. 0.8 x 0.008 = _____

34. 206.08 ÷ 64 = _____   39. 396 ÷ 8.8 = _____

35. 130 x 3.3 = _____   40. –30.8 ÷ 4 = _____

Name _____

41–45: Change the fractions to decimals and the decimals to fractions. (Round decimal answers to the nearest hundredth.)

41. $\frac{3}{5}$ = _____

42. 10.75 = _____

43. $\frac{22}{25}$ = _____

44. 0.625 = _____

45. $3\frac{5}{7}$ = _____

46–47: Write these as whole numbers.

46. 2.7×10^6 = _____

47. 8.95×10^8 = _____

48–49: Write these in scientific notation.

48. 73,420,000 = _____

49. 9,561,000 = _____

50–58: Write the decimals as percents and the percents as decimals.

50. 0.532 = _____

51. 36.5 = _____

52. 6.992 = _____

53. 83.6% = _____

54. 205.3% = _____

55. 1.03% = _____

56. 13% = _____

57. 0.17 = _____

58. 55.5% = _____

59–64: Fill in the blanks with the missing numbers.

59. 2.25 is _____% of 45.

60. 48 is _____% of 300.

61. _____ is 25% of 38.

62. _____ is 140% of 60.6.

63. 170 is 85% of _____

64. 37.5 is 5% of _____

65–70: Change each fraction into a decimal. Write R or T to show whether the decimal is repeating (R) or terminating (T).

T / R   T / R   T / R   T / R   T / R   T / R

65._____   66._____   67._____   68._____   69._____   70. _____

Name _____

MORE! Basic Skills/Decimals 6-8+

71–75: 6 points each

Solve these problems. Round decimal answers to the nearest hundredth.

71. Each member of Judo Team A drinks 4.35 L of water during each competition. Team A has 16 members. Team B drinks 7.62 L less than Team A at each competition. How much does Team B drink?

    *Answer:*_____

74. Basketball player Joe had an average of 1.5 steals per game in his last 50 games. This average was 5 times the stealing average of Moe in the same 50 games. How many steals did Moe have?

    *Answer:*_____

72. After a long practice session, Gonzo the weightlifter ate 3 hamburgers, 2 slices of pizza, 2 orders of fries, 1 salad, and 2 large drinks. The restaurant added 5% tax to his bill, and Gonzo left a 15% tip. What was the total cost? *(Calculate the tip on the total of the food costs without the tax added.)*

    *Answer:*_____

75. A free diver dove to 48 feet below the surface of the ocean. From there she rose up in the water 36.5 feet. What was her position then (in relation to the surface of the water)?

    *Answer:*_____

73. Baseball player Adam signed a contract for $1,450,000 a year. Another player, Pete, signed a contract for 115% of the amount of Adam's contract. How much is Pete's salary per year?

    *Answer:*_____

Menu

hamburger......$4.95

pizza slice......$3.10

fries.............$2.50

salad............$3.95

drinks (lg.)......$1.90

Total Score _____ points (of 100 possible)

Name

DECIMALS
SKILLS TEST ANSWER KEY

1. B

2. H

3. G

4. E

5. J

6. 5.05

7. 55.5

8. 2.006

9. 0.063

10. 0.89

11. 0.00014

12. seven hundred-thousandths

13. one hundred four thousandths

14. seventeen and three hundredths

15. ten-thousandths

16. ones

17. hundredths

18. hundred-thousandths

19. tens

20. thousandths

21. 75.4

22. 75.369

23. 80

24. 75.37

25. 75

26. <

27. >

28. =

29. >

30. 6.006, 6.06, 6.061, 6.106, 6.16

31. 186

32. 3.335

33. –35.1

34. 3.22

35. 429

36. 0.9536

37. 4292

38. 0.0064

39. 45

40. –7.7

41. 0.6

42. $10\frac{3}{4}$

43. 0.88

44. $\frac{5}{8}$

45. 3.71

46. 2,700,000

47. 895,000,000

48. 7.342×10^7

49. 9.561×10^6

50. 53.2%

51. 3650%

52. 699.2%

53. 0.836

54. 2.053

55. 0.0103

56. 0.13

57. 17%

58. 0.555

59. 5%

60. 16%

61. 9.5

62. 84.84

63. 200

64. 750

65. R, $0.6\overline{6}$

66. T, 0.875

67. T, 0.8

68. R, $0.4\overline{4}$

69. R, $0.416\overline{6}$

70. T, 0.64

71. 61.98 L

72. 40.56

73. $1,667,500

74. 15

75. –11.5 ft

ANSWERS

page 10

1. c
2. d
3. a
4. c
5. a
6. b

page 11

1. e
2. g
3. c
4. f
5. h
6. a
7. b
8. d
9. m
10. p
11. j
12. s
13. q
14. i
15. n

page 12

1. 45.66
2. 73.25
3. 6.2016
4. 8.865
5. 12.69
6. 15.8
7. 7.27
8. 0.516
9. 0.003
10. 0.0005
11. 0.062
12. 0.00011
13. 0.934
14. 0.89
15. 0.08
16. 0.00009
17. 0.0209
18. 0.6002

page 13

1. four and three thousand, three hundred, thirty-three ten-thousandths
2. one hundred thirty-six thousandths
3. three and sixty-seven hundredths
4. three and nine tenths
5. ninety-one hundredths
6. seven tenths
7. four hundred thirty-six thousandths
8. two hundred-thousandths
9. one hundred one ten-thousandths
10. two thousand twenty-two ten-thousandths
11. sixty-six hundredths
12. eight thousandths

page 14

1. no
2. no
3. yes
4. no
5. no
6. b
7. c

page 15

1. c
2. c
3. b
4. a
5. c
6. c
7. a
8. c
9. b
10. a

page 16

1. $1.089 < 1.909$
2. $0.92 > 0.909$
3. $1.88 < 1.9$
4. $0.99 > 0.919$
5. $0.0099 < 1.07$
6. $1.09 = 1.09$
7. $1.089 < 1.09$
8. $1.9 = 1.90$

page 17

1. VA, JL, CT, RR, TM
2. JL, RR, CT, VA, TM
3. CT, JL, RR, VA, TM
4. CT, VA, TM, JL, RR
5. CT, VA, JL, TM, RR
6. D
7. G
8. E

page 18

1. hundredths
2. thousandths
3. tenths
4. tenths
5. thousandths
6. hundred-thousandths
7. hundredths
8. thousandths
9. thousands
10. tenths
11. ones
12. tenths
13. ten-thousandths
14. hundreds

page 19

1. thousandths
2. hundredths
3. ten
4. thousandths
5. tenths
6. hundredths
7. ones
8. hundreds
9. tenths
10. tens
11. ten-thousandths
12. ten-thousandths
13. tenths
14. ones
15. ones; tenths

page 20

1. 57.82
2. 57.8
3. 60
4. 9.2
5. 170
6. 167.37
7. 9.8192
8. 54.55

page 21

1. 4.22; 4.216
2. 1; 1.5
3. 2.76; 2.8
4. 5.96; 6
5. 0.37; 0.4
6. 1.790; 1.79
7. 1.05; 1.1
8. 0.705; 1
9. 0.2407; 0.241

page 22

A. 2.6424
B. 26.053
C. 67.183
D. 7,552.407
E. 25.3019
F. 7,005.4006
G. 1.9998
H. 66.8016
I. 1.4313
J. 1.169
K. 110.163

page 23

1. 1.095 mph
2. 15.956 mph
3. 0.966 sec
4. 1,908.756 km
5. 36.337 yrs
6. 1.73 m
7. 5.55 m
8. 16.637 mi

page 24

1. 0.377/sec
2. 0.488/sec
3. 2.25 hr
4. 86.1 min
5. 176
6. 477
7. 39
8. 126
9. 2.392 L
10. 16.74 ft^2

page 25

Week 2 – 42 min
Week 3 – 46 min
Week 4 – 50 min
Week 5 – 60 min
Week 6 – 64 min
1. b
2. b
3. b
4. c
5. c
6. a
7. b
8. d

page 26

1. 3.22
2. 45
3. 3.5
4. 55.5
5. 8.23
6. 0.07

page 27

TOM
1. 0.24
2. 122
3. yes
4. 11
5. 6.8
AMY
1. yes
2. 116
3. 6.7
4. 33
5. 9.2

page 28

1. 103 kg
2. 150.166 kg
3. 262 kg
4. 52 kg
5. 1,092 hr
6. 20.66 mi
7. 1,139.55 calories
8. 28,702 mi
9. 341,900
10. 7,000
11. 6,666,660
12. 5,663.2

page 29

1. 4.003
2. 9.2
3. 61.7526
4. 12.7215
5. 0.361
6. 0.045
7. 0.00055
8. 2.20075
9. 319.662
10. 4.00032
11. 8.8888
12. 11.09887
13. 0.002951
14. 0.00999
15. 0.00005
16. 0.6521198
17. 0.0001
18. 0.03003

page 30

1. 5.106 m/sec
2. 3.769 ft/sec
3. 9.822 sec
4. 1,347 rolls
5. 4.641 m/sec
6. 0.522
7. 2.609 sec

page 31

1. 5.394 m/sec
2. 5.923 m/sec
3. 33.12 seconds
4. 18.75 sec difference; slower
5. 155.5 lbs
6. 1 min, 5.18 sec or 1:5.18
7. 11,025 m

page 32

1. −489.8 ft
2. 2.2
3. 16.5
4. 67.7
5. −15.4
6. −12.265
7. −29.3
8. 25.3
9. −22.9
10. 1
11. −101.101
12. 808.3
13. 9.9

page 33

1. $5 \times 0.6 = 3$
2. $-10.9 + 26.7 = 15.8$ ft
3. $-3.6 \times 0.5 = -1.8$ ft
4. $95.35 \div 5 = 19.07$ ft
5. $-8.6 + (-1.9) = -10.5$ ft
6. $-11.4 - (-3.7) = -7.7$ ft

page 34

1. 2.6×10^7
2. 5.9×10^9

3. 1.496×10^8
4. 4.73×10^6
5. 8.5×10^{10}
6. 1.6×10^4
7. 9.876×10^8
8. 3.7×10^9
9. 6.66×10^6
10. 2.22×10^5
11. 9.09×10^{11}

page 35

1. 90,900,000
2. 1,220,000
3. 611,000
4. 1,100,000,000
5. 81,230,000
6. 50,300
7. 3,800,000
8. 7,625,000,000,000
9. 44,400,000,000

page 36

A. 4.02
B. 6.14
C. 0.25
D. 0.8
E. 25.75
F. 0.4
G. 0.625
H. 10.6
I. 0.438
J. 0.667
K. 0.917
L. 0.556
M. 4.833
N. 10.667
O. 25.714
P. 4.875
Q. 25.778

page 37

1. $71\frac{27}{50}$ m
2. $23\frac{3}{25}$ m
3. $22\frac{63}{100}$ m
4. $76\frac{4}{5}$ m
5. $74\frac{2}{25}$ m
6. $86\frac{37}{50}$ m
7. $98\frac{12}{25}$ m
8. $8\frac{4}{5}$ m
9. $7\frac{13}{50}$ m
10. $3\frac{3}{4}$ m
11. $2\frac{1}{2}$ m

Countries are: Cuba, USA, USSR

page 38

A. 10.7%
B. 0.055
C. 6.9%
D. 9.4%
E. 15%
F. 0.088
G. 9.6%
H. 0.175
I. 0.04
J. 12.5%
1. 0.2
2. 200%

3. 11.1%
4. 0.1
5. 2.67
6. 16.6%
7. 0.133

page 39

a. 57.2%
b. 0.691
c. 0.4611
d. 2.35
e. 181.5%
f. 0.0094
g. 0.02
h. 5.525%
i. 0.966
j. 0.00034
k. 0.831
l. 0.838
m. 57.622%
n. 1,634,020%
o. 440%
p. 9999%
q. 8.0

page 40

1. 16.7%
2. 50%
3. 16.7%
4. 42.9%
5. 75
6. 100
7. 25
8. 451
9. no
10. 192
11. yes
12. 140.76

page 41

1. 94
2. 65%
3. 328
4. 900
5. 1%
6. 275%
7. 300,000
8. 552
9. 180
10. 35%

page 42

1. 3,500%
2. b
3. 61.7 %
4. 3,768,650
5. 75%
6. a
7. 20,250
8. 0.0429% or 0.043%
9. 678

page 43

1. 87,500
2. 24.4% (approx)
3. 24,640
4. 104,000
5. 58%
6. 104,125
7. 15%
8. 68%

page 44

Answers may vary somewhat.
Brad: $21.66 (Subt. $17.90, tip $2.69, tax $1.07)
Fred: $36.66 (Subt. $30.30, tip $4.54, tax $1.82)
Ted: $36.42 (Subt. $30.10, tip $4.51, tax $1.81)
Tad: $39.20 (Subt. $32.40, tip $4.86, tax $1.94)
Chad: $40.53 (Subt. $33.50, tip $5.03, tax $2.01)

page 45

A. $909.50
B. $1,110.00
C. 3 years
D. 6%
E. $750
F. $41,250
G. $2,200.00

page 46

1. $158.00
2. $170.25
3. $151.20
4. $104.00
5. $126.00
6. $1,674.00
7. $1,125.60

page 47

1. $3,325,000
2. $12,452,479.50
3. $19,612,988
4. $1,200,000
5. $4,266,097.50
6. $460,349.50
7. $34,291,770
8. $80,300,000
9. $25,200,000
10. $8,100,000

page 48

1. T
2. R
3. T $0.187\overline{5}$
4. R $0.06\overline{6}$
5. R $0.2\overline{2}$
6. T   0.4
7. T   0.45
8. T   0.3125
9. T   0.28
10. T $0.4\overline{8}$
11. R $0.83\overline{3}$
12. T   0.625